THE DYNAMIC DUO AND THE SUPERPOWER OF KINDNESS

By Nancy Franklin-Wright

Kindness is a gift that can be given over and over again!

~Nancy Franklin-Wright

THE DYNAMIC DUO AND THE SUPERPOWER OF KINDNESS

ISBN: 978-1-7363609-7-2 (Paperback)

Library of Congress Cataloging-in-Publication data is on file with the publisher.

Visit www.authornfranklinwright.com

THE DYNAMIC DUO AND THE SUPERPOWER OF KINDNESS

By Nancy Franklin-Wright

Kindness is a superpower.

Some may say, "No way. How is that possible ?"

Oh, it's **possible**. Let the Dynamic Duo show you the way.

Being kind to **yourself** is easy when you do your best and are willing to **learn** how to do even better.

When you are kind to yourself
you can do many **things**.

Take a few **deep breaths** to **calm** down when something doesn't go your way.

Go to your room and play with your toys or read a **funny** book to **laugh** your worries away.

Take a moment to think about how your amazing brain will choose to react to your feelings.

Will it cause you or another person to feel pain?

When you show kindness toward yourself you can **make** your dark clouds turn blue.

You have the superpower of kindness to **help** you.

Showing kindness toward your family is a wonderful thing to do. Offering to help Mom prepare dinner always makes her smile.

Sharing my toys with my little sister really makes her day.

She gives me a great big hug and tells me I'm the best!

Kindness is a superpower.
Let us show you more of what it **can** do.

Having friends to play with is lots of fun.

It's always best to be kind to them, especially when they feel sad.

A high five or a hug goes a long way. Because of kindness, your friends will always be around.

You can show kindness toward a new kid in your school by offering to sit with them at lunchtime so they don't feel lonely. It will make you both feel great, and you might make a new friend!

It's so cool to use the superpower of **kindness**.

Pets are also great to have around. They like to give kisses, licks, and cuddles all the time .

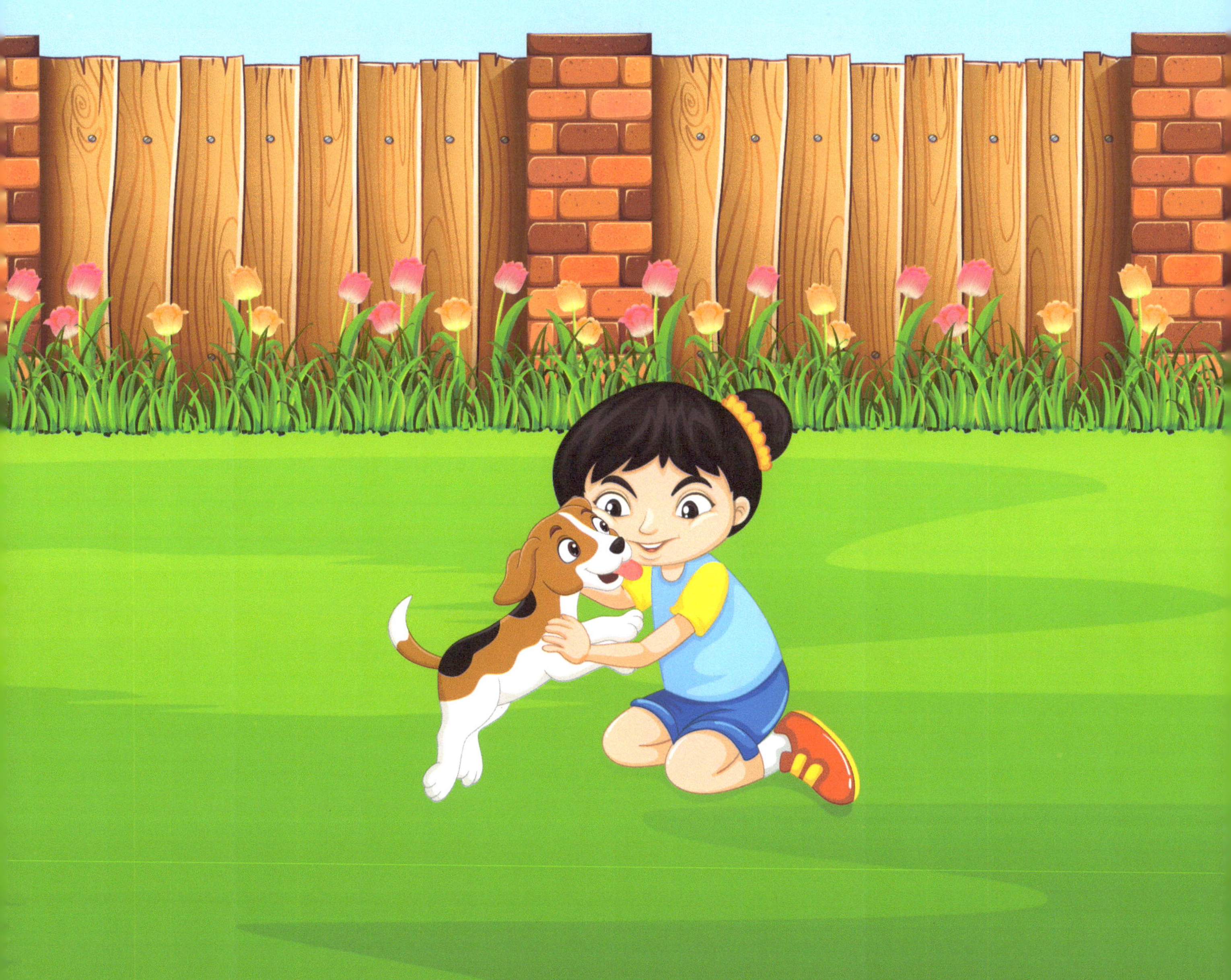

The love and care we show to our pets only make their **loyalty** and **love** for us grow stronger.

We are kind to our pets because kindness saves the day.

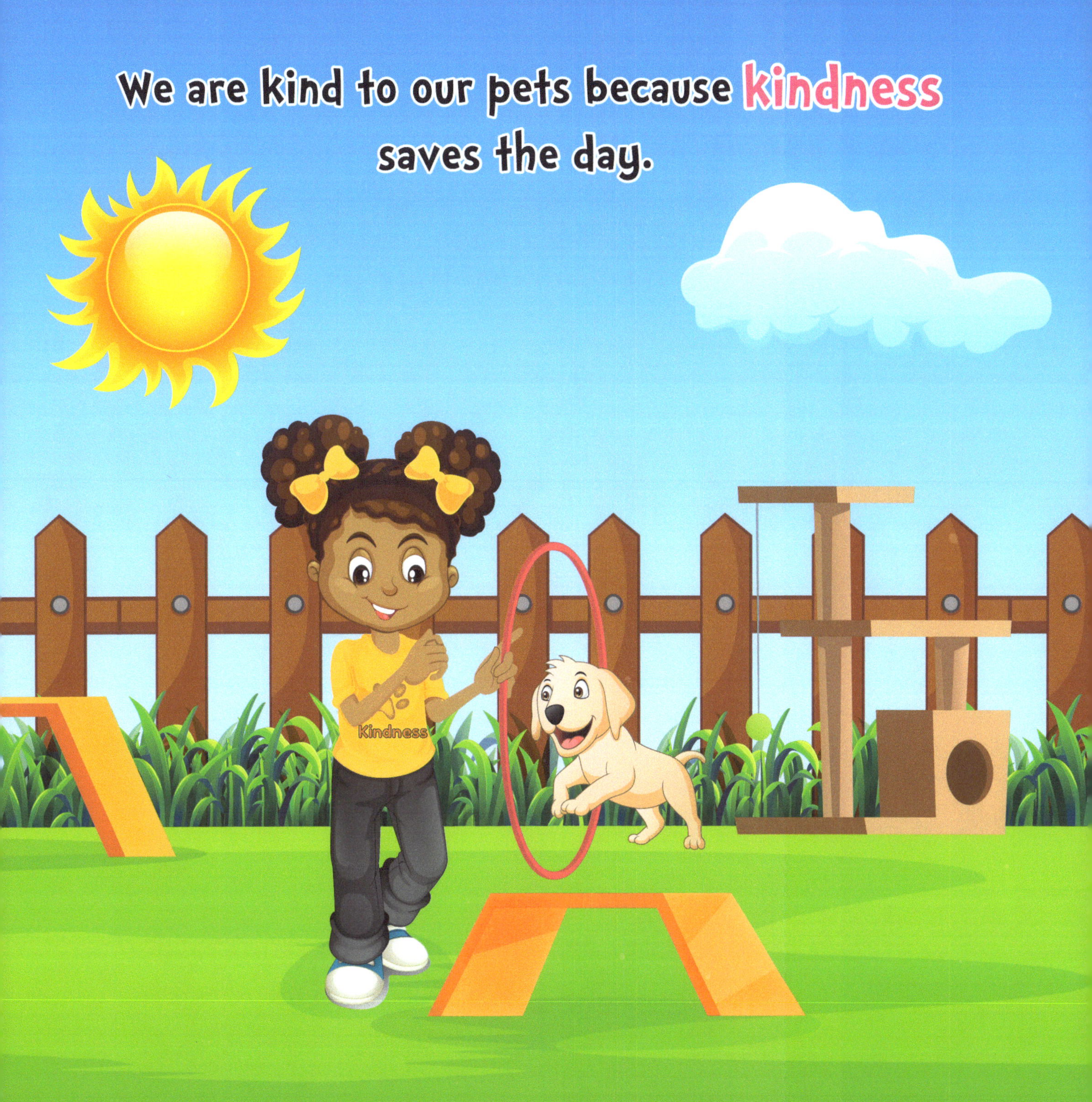

Every person we see is **unique**.
Some people we see may be short or tall.
They may have curly hair, straight hair, red hair, blue hair, or no hair at all .

They may like to wear **different** clothes than us.

Even though we all have differences, we are still kind to others .

Kindness is a superpower, you say?

The Dynamic Duo has something to prove. You, too, can use the superpower of **kindness** to change your world .

Can you unleash your superpower of **kindness**?

Nancy Franklin-Wright is a talented children's book author, who's reputable for her great passion for empowering young girls with great value to grow into confident, responsible, and focused adults. Nancy has a vast wealth or experience working with children as a volunteer and in a paid position. She is the founder of the D.I.V.A's (Daring, Inspired, Victorious, Awesome) Club, which focuses on helping girls of ages 6-12 to develop leadership skills, enhance their self-esteem, and other positive character traits.

Nancy's competency while working with children lies in her great sense of focus and the array of highly engaging, versatile, and effective methods that she uses to coach them. She holds a Bachelor's degree in Healthcare Administration, a Master's (with honors) in Human Resource Management and has taken an undergraduate course in Introduction to Education.

In her spare time, Nancy enjoys spending quality time with her family and friends, baking, eating good food, reading, exercising, photography, and singing.

www.ingramcontent.com/pod-product-compliance
Lightning Source LLC
LaVergne TN
LVHW070205110826
845147LV00002B/509

* 9 7 8 1 7 3 6 3 6 0 9 6 5 *